SPECIAL NOTE TO PARENTS

Thank you for purchasing *The Shoes: Parent's Guide.* We hope you and your child have a rewarding time and experience engaging in this interactive book. The Shoes-Parent Edition provides an exciting opportunity for open dialogue between you and your child about things that may affect children's self-esteem, social abilities, or learning!

Dr. Kenneth R. Gay, Jr.
Founder, Kenneth Gay Education, LLC
kennethgayeducation.com

WIN THE DAY!

KENNETHGAYEDUCATION.COM | @ 2022 KENNETH GAY EDUCATION, LLC

TABLE OF CONTENT

TITLE	PAGE#
PREFACE	1
HOW TO USE THIS BOOK	5
SECTION 1: THE SHOES	7
SECTION 2: SOCIAL-EMOTIONAL LEARNING (SEL)	13
SECTION 3: PARENT STRATEGIES	19
SECTION 4: TIPS FROM PARENTS JUST LIKE YOU	33
SECTION 5: PARENT/CHILD ACTIVITY-DESIGN YOUR FAVORITE PAIR	47
REFERENCES & CLOSING	71

KENNETHGAYEDUCATION.COM | @ 2022 KENNETH GAY EDUCATION, LLC

THE SHOES

PARENT'S GUIDE
STUDENT SOCIAL-EMOTIONAL LEARNING
THROUGH STORYTELLING

DR. KENNETH R. GAY, JR.

Copyright @ 2022 Kenneth Gay Education, LLC
All rights reserved.
ISBN: 9798848031140

PREFACE

Dr. Kenneth Gay was born in Lake Charles, Louisiana. Raised in a two-parent household, his mother was an educator and worked as a speech therapist, later becoming a school board member in his hometown. His father was an accountant at a chemical plant for many years and an entrepreneur with several successful businesses. He grew up with one sibling, his sister, who later became an educator.

Dr. Gay grew up in an African American community, exposed to drugs, alcohol, and sometimes violence. While not wealthy, he was fortunate to grow up having a positive male role model, and he could see the adverse effects on his peers who did not have one. His home was one of the largest in their neighborhood and became a safe place where everyone felt welcome. There could easily be 20 young men on any given day playing basketball.

Dr. Gay never considered himself to be better than any of his friends. He knew he had the advantages of having strong faith in Christ and knowing that he could look to his parents for guidance and mentorship. As a result, Dr. Gay never did drugs or alcohol. Admittedly, he was always paranoid about not being in total control of his emotions, thoughts, and actions.

PREFACE

Over the past two decades, Dr. Gay has had the opportunity to serve as an educator. He began his career as an elementary teacher, later as an elementary and high school assistant principal, and then a high school principal. His career has culminated as an executive Director of Administration, working in Central Office. With less than 2% of African American males working in education, one would almost consider this an anomaly.

One unique aspect of his career as an educator, he has simultaneously served over 27 years in the Army Reserves. His experience in the Army Reserves began as an enlisted Soldier and later he received his commissioning as an officer. He held various leadership roles, such as company commander, branch chief, and battalion commander. As a result, he could use his educational leadership skills in various military capacities, deliver instructions, and use military techniques in education. His dual career has aided him tremendously in academic operations, communication, and working with different teams in large organizations.

PREFACE

He now sees the advantages of the military and the field of education. Combined with a love of entrepreneurship, it has allowed him to see a future as a CEO, working towards moving a company in the right direction. With these experiences as a CEO, educator, military veteran, and parent of an adult child, he is excited to share some of his experiences.

HOW TO USE THIS BOOK

WELCOME!

Thank you for embarking on this journey. Parenting can be the most rewarding thing and then, on the other hand, the scariest thing. Our kids don't come with manuals. If we could buy one, it would surely be the world's best seller. Our students' happiness, education, safety, and success fall upon us as parents, educators, and community members.

This book features the short story, <u>The Shoes</u>. The story is about the real-life events of the author Dr. Kenneth R. Gay Jr., and features lessons he learned during his career as an elementary school teacher. This story lays the foundation for teaching students how to empathize with others. It also addresses the concept of respect and explores aspects of peer pressure. The activities, tips, topics, and resources came from people like you. They felt inspired to share their knowledge, greatest hopes, successes, and missteps.

Please take a moment to read the story. So many other concepts are present in this story. As you read the story, think about ideas you could share with your children. Also, take moments to write in the margins and highlight as needed.

Throughout the book, you will find activities, tips, topics, and resources to help you engage with your children at home and in the community. Importantly, it will encourage you to build strong partnerships with educators. Please allow this book to help you strengthen your bond with your children, educators, and community members.

WIN THE DAY!

SECTION 1:
THE SHOES

THE SHOES

I remember beginning my first year in education as a new teacher going into one of the most challenging schools in my school district. An apartment complex directly cattycorner to the school was one of the toughest to live in all of Houston, Texas. I could remember the nervousness I felt before the first days of school. Being a recent college graduate, I wanted to make sure I looked a little bit older than my age. I would meet students for the first time in my fourth-grade class. Of course, all the education, theory, and practices are very relevant or very good. Still, until you step foot in the classroom for the first time and have time to work on your practical skills, that's when the real lessons begin. I remember the first day of school when the students came. I tried to put on my best face to look very serious and stern. "Hey, do not smile until the end of your first year," veteran teachers and mentors advised. I just wanted to make it to December because I knew I'd at least be halfway through my school year. My biggest goal was to ensure my students were successful despite my first year as a teacher. I thought I was there to teach but it surprised me how much the students taught me. I have carried those valuable lessons throughout my career.

THE SHOES

I can remember it, like yesterday. One Thursday in October, I saw some students laugh and talk in hushed voices. I was trying to figure out precisely why all the giggling and laughing. They weren't very disruptive, but I wanted to figure out what was happening. Slyly and keenly observing, I discovered they were laughing at a student's shoes. Even though 90% of the students probably lived in poverty, they were still laughing at the student's shoes. Luckily for me, I knew what was going on. I grew up in an African American community where even if you were living in poverty, one way that students ranked themselves as being a little bit better than others was by their shoes. Let me break it down for you. Students may not be able to afford a car to drive, but your shoes are basically like a car. It was a way of showing that you have status, class, and style.

The student they were making fun of was laughing too. But I could see from his expressions that he was uncomfortable in the situation. So, I continued to watch, and I had the most challenging time in the world, taking my mind off this situation.

THE SHOES

I truly enjoyed working at an elementary school because we could wear college or university polo shirts with some jeans on Fridays. Considering myself to be young and fresh out of college, I thought I was cool. At the time, FUBU (For Us By Us), an African American company, made jeans popular with the Fat Albert-themed character. Yes, I used to think I was super cool. I was "Mr. Teacher" because I wore nice jeans and sneakers on Fridays. However, when I left school that day, I couldn't take my mind off the student who felt so uncomfortable. So, I went to one of the local thrift stores to find shoes similar to the ones the student was wearing. I had an idea of what the shoes should look like, but I was not very optimistic that I would find them. They needed to look like bowling shoes. They had some that didn't have shoelaces; they had straps, to my amazement. I purchased the $5 shoes, got to the car, and put them on. I had to put my shoes to the test. My next stop was the mall. As I walked through the mall with confidence and glory, I remember hearing a group of young African American ladies say, "He's cute, but man, what kind of shoes does this guy have on?" In that moment, I knew I had made the right choice.

THE SHOES

The following day, I was so excited. I dressed in my FUBU Fat Albert jeans and my brand new $5 shoes with the straps. You could have heard a rat running on cotton that day. When the students arrived, they looked in astonishment! For whatever reason, the students loved to see how their principals and teachers dressed on Fridays. That day I decided to open the lesson on how your current situation would not be your situation tomorrow. If you work hard and engage yourself, you have endless possibilities when you grow up. I decided not to take a story from my life because I was fortunate enough to have my father, but told the story from my father that he had shared about some shoes that I would never forget.

I shared what my father told - me when he was a young boy growing up very poor, he had shoes given to him that two or three other people had previously worn. The shoes were often two sizes too big, and his grandmother would have to put tissue inside of his shoes for them to have a snug fit on my father's feet. Because the shoes were so raggedy, his grandmother used to tape the shoes and spray black paint over the tape at night while he was asleep.

THE SHOES

He shared that some students at school often made fun of him because he did not have new shoes. However, his grandmother told him he might not have new shoes right now. But if you work hard, be kind to people, even when people mistreat you, that one day you'll be able to purchase the type of shoes you want. So, my dad did just that. As a result, he was the first in his family to go to college, graduate, and become an accountant.

I shared with the students that sometimes people experience different circumstances in life. For example, you can look around the city and see that some people are poor and some are rich. I shared with them it didn't matter if you started poor. One day, you can become rich. You may even begin rich and one day become poor.

In closing, "the shoes" I purchased twenty years ago for $5 made a major impact on my educational and military careers. I learned never to judge anyone based on their shoes or financial status. When students have knowledge and self-awareness, I realized they could learn to love themselves and empathize with others.

SECTION 2:
SOCIAL- EMOTIONAL LEARNING

SOCIAL-EMOTIONAL LEARNING

> "When students have knowledge and self-awareness, I realized they could learn to love themselves and empathize with others.
> -Dr. Kenneth R. Gay, Jr."

What words, phrases, or thoughts come to mind when you think **social** and **emotional**? Those words aren't always used together. Write your thoughts here.

SOCIAL-EMOTIONAL LEARNING

According to the Collaborative for Academic, Social, and Emotional Learning (CASEL),

SEL

SOCIAL-EMOTIONAL LEARNING

"is an **integral part of education** and **human development**. SEL is the process through which all young people and adults acquire and apply the knowledge, skills, and attitudes to **develop healthy identities**, **manage emotions** and **achieve personal** and **collective goals**, feel and show **empathy** for others, establish and maintain supportive **relationships**, and make **responsible** and **caring decisions**."
https://casel.org/fundamentals-of-sel/

SOCIAL-EMOTIONAL LEARNING

Since the global pandemic and subsequent lockdowns, Social-Emotional Learning (SEL) and the well-being of youth deserve the spotlight now more than ever.

Social-Emotional Learning (SEL) is important because it provides the groundwork for impactful, positive, and meaningful learning.

Social-Emotional Learning helps students develop crucial, lifelong skills. Listed below are just a few examples of thoes skills.

- Self Awareness
- Self Management
- Stress Management
- Identifying Triggers
- Resilience
- Emotional Awareness
- Social Awareness
- Responsible Decision Making
- Self Control
- Confidence
- Independence
- Peer Pressure
- Compassion
- Values
- Empathy

NOTE: Which SEL words are related to key concepts from the story "The Shoes"?

SOCIAL-EMOTIONAL LEARNING

WHAT'S YOUR TEMPERATURE?

The number one method of helping our children is to model the behaviors we want them to have. Take a moment a do an honest assessment by gauging the temperature of your behavior and beliefs.

Maybe there are some areas that you could improve. For example, it could be that you have difficulty expressing your feelings, or perhaps you allow someone to take advantage of your kindness.

No matter what the situation, our children are always watching and learning.

Write your thoughts here.

SECTION 3:
PARENT STRATEGIES

POSITIVE IMPACTS OF SOCIAL-EMOTIONAL LEARNING

According to the The Organization for Economic Co-operation and Development (OECD) Survey on Social and Emotional Skills, SEL has positive impact on many factor that impact an individual's ability to thrive and achieve life satisfaction.

What are your thoughts about how SEL impact both present and future issues?

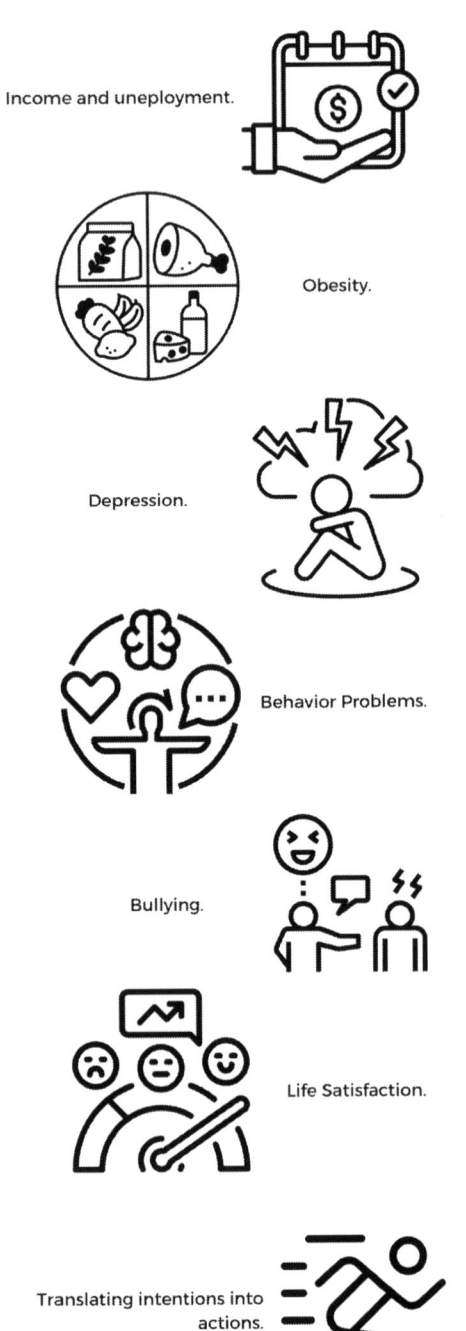

- Attendance and completion of higher education.
- Income and uneployment.
- Obesity.
- Depression.
- Behavior Problems.
- Bullying.
- Life Satisfaction.
- Translating intentions into actions.

KENNETHGAYEDUCATION.COM | @ 2022 KENNETH GAY EDUCATION, LLC

IMPROVING YOUR CHILD'S SOCIAL EMOTIONAL LEARNING SKILLS

REMINDER: Social and emotional intelligence is the awareness of and ability to manage one's emotions and empathize with others.

The key concepts are Self-Regulation, Self-Awareness, and Social Skills. By honing in on these three areas, you can significantly impact your child's overall Social and Emotional Learning Skills.

Self-Regulation
- Identify triggers
- Name your emotions
- Practice healthy living
- Stay connected with friends

Self-Awareness
- Identify early attachment experiences that may have influenced how you currently manage your emotions
- Practice mindfulness to connect with your emotions
- Ask for feedback

Social Skills
- Identify nonverbal cues in others
- Practice active listening skills
- Empathize with others

Think about how each concept impacts day-to-day activities and your child's ability to be successful in a variety of settings?

IMPROVING YOUR CHILD'S
SOCIAL EMOTIONAL LEARNING SKILLS THROUGH
SELF-REGULATION

Self-Regulation

Parents play a big role in helping their child learn how to identify and cope with emotions. Through social emotional learning, youth learn how to understand and regulate emotions. This helps them to develop self-regulation skills, which are essential for achieving success in school and in life.

Parents can support their child's social emotional learning by providing opportunities for them to practice identifying and expressing emotions. For example, parents can ask their child how they are feeling after a tough day at school or during a family conflict. By providing opportunities for emotions to be acknowledged and addressed, parents can help their child develop the skills necessary for healthy emotional development.

More specifically, parents can assist their children:

- Identify triggers
- Name emotions
- Practice healthy living
- Stay connected with friends

The next few pages provide material and sample resources that will help you assist your child with identifying and naming their emotions and identifying triggers.

How does your role as a parent or guardian effect how your children express and regulate their emotions?

IMPROVING YOUR CHILD'S SOCIAL EMOTIONAL LEARNING SKILLS THROUGH SELF-REGULATION

MEET YOUR MOOD METER

The mood meter shows us that everyone has a variety of emotions or feelings. They can range from positive to negative and from low energy to high energy.

ENERGY (High → Low) vs **PLEASANTNESS** (Neg → Pos)

High Energy / Negative:
- enraged
- furious
- angry
- irritated

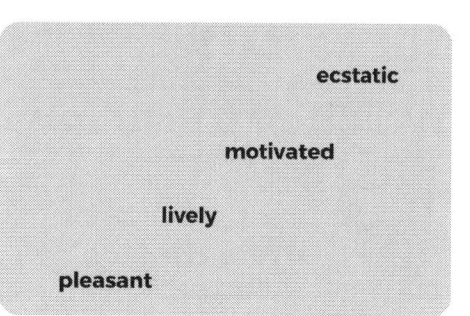

High Energy / Positive:
- ecstatic
- motivated
- lively
- pleasant

Low Energy / Negative:
- apathetic
- lonely
- exhausted
- despair

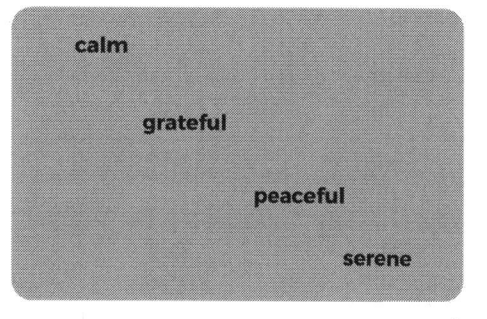

Low Energy / Positive:
- calm
- grateful
- peaceful
- serene

TIP: Identifying where our feelings are in the meter can help us find ways on how to address them. For example, if we have a negative emotion that is in high energy, we can think of ways to calm down and move away from thinking negatively. We can do this for ourselves or even to help out a friend or a family member.

ANNOYED	FOND	LIVELY	SKITTISH
ANXIOUS	FRIENDLY	LONELY	SULLEN
CHEERFUL	GLAD	MISTREATED	THOUGHTFUL
CHERISHING	HELPLESS	MORTIFIED	THRILLED
DEFEATED	HOPEFUL	OSTRACIZED	UNCOMFORTABLE
DEFENSIVE	INCOMPLETE	OUTRAGED	UNSURE
DISTRACTED	INFERIOR	REGRETFUL	WORRIED
ECSTATIC	INTIMIDATED	REJECTED	WITHDRAWN

Sources:
https://www.ps120q.org/mood-meter
https://tomdrummond.com/app/uploads/2019/11/Emotion-Feelings.pdf

KENNETHGAYEDUCATION.COM | @ 2022 KENNETH GAY EDUCATION, LLC

IMPROVING YOUR CHILD'S SOCIAL EMOTIONAL LEARNING SKILLS THROUGH SELF-REGULATION

TIP: Help your child identify triggers that stir anger and other emotions. Use this worksheet as a guide to help them remember things that trigger positive and negative responses.

IDENTIFYING TRIGGERS

Which of the following makes you feel angry?

- [ ] Someone says you did something wrong.
- [ ] Someone belittles you.
- [ ] You want something you cannot have.
- [ ] Someone shouts at you.
- [ ] You are told you can't do something right.
- [ ] Someone doesn't agree with you.
- [ ] You are unable to finish your task.
- [ ] You are feeling left out.
- [ ] There's too many people.
- [ ] There's too much noise.
- [ ] Someone is disturbing you.
- [ ] There's too much homework.
- [ ] There's too much housework.
- [ ] Someone criticizes you.
- [ ] Someone hurts you.
- [ ] Someone threatens you.

KENNETHGAYEDUCATION.COM | @ 2022 KENNETH GAY EDUCATION, LLC

IMPROVING YOUR CHILD'S
SOCIAL EMOTIONAL LEARNING SKILLS THROUGH
SELF-REGULATION

TIP: Use this worksheet to help your child identify tools they can use to cope with different situations.

COPING TOOLS
WHAT HELPS ME

- [ ] Take slow, mindful breaths
- [ ] Drink a warm cup of water
- [ ] Rest and take a break
- [ ] Stretch
- [ ] Journal or write a letter
- [ ] Listen to your favorite music
- [ ] Talk to someone you trust
- [ ] Get a hug
- [ ] Cuddle or play with your pet
- [ ] Use positive affirmations
- [ ] Use a stress ball
- [ ] Blow bubbles
- [ ] Make an artwork
- [ ] Hug or climb a tree
- [ ] Read a book or magazine
- [ ] Take a shower or bath

KENNETHGAYEDUCATION.COM | @ 2022 KENNETH GAY EDUCATION, LLC

IMPROVING YOUR CHILD'S
SOCIAL EMOTIONAL LEARNING SKILLS THROUGH
SELF-AWARENESS

Self-Awareness

Parents play a vital role in helping their child develop self-awareness. One way they can do this is by modeling mindfulness themselves. This means being present in the moment and aware of your own thoughts, emotions, and behaviors. It also involves being accepting of yourself, warts and all. When parents are mindful, their children learn that it's okay to be imperfect and that mistakes are part of the human experience.

They also learn the importance of paying attention to their inner experiences and treating themselves with kindness and compassion. In addition to modeling mindfulness, parents can also help their child develop self-awareness by teaching them social emotional learning skills. These skills involve things like recognizing and managing emotions, setting boundaries, and resolving conflict. By teaching these skills to their child, parents can help them develop a greater understanding of themselves and the world around them.

Parents can assist their children with the following:

- Identify early attachment experiences that may have influenced how you currently manage your emotions
- Practice mindfulness to connect with your emotions
- Ask for feedback

The next few pages provide material and sample resources that will help you assist your child with identifying and naming their emotions and identifying triggers.

How does your role as a parent or guardian effect how your children develop self-awareness skills?

IMPROVING YOUR CHILD'S
SOCIAL EMOTIONAL LEARNING SKILLS THROUGH
SELF-AWARENESS

TIP: Use this handy guide to help your child quickly identify areas they can be grateful for throughout their day. For example, this one uses the phrase, how many "thank-you's" did you say today? You can also ask your child to observe how many smiles or compliments they gave or were given.

Guide to Mindful Gratitude in two steps

01 Start by observing. How many thank you's did you say today? How are you feeling when you express thanks?

02 Recall the instance you said thanks today. What were you grateful for?

IMPROVING YOUR CHILD'S
SOCIAL EMOTIONAL LEARNING SKILLS THROUGH
SELF-AWARENESS

TIP: The Mindful Habits Formula is just a quick guide to help your child develop healthy habits of setting boundaries, telling the truth, and listening to their intuition. Many of these tips go a long way in preventing bullying and resisting peer pressure.

Mindful Habits
Formula

- Setting Boundaries ✓
- Deep Breathing ✓
- Telling The Truth ✓
- Engaging In honest Convos ✓
- Listening To Intuition ✓

Look Inside *Maintain Balance*

IMPROVING YOUR CHILD'S
SOCIAL EMOTIONAL LEARNING SKILLS THROUGH
SOCIAL SKILLS

Social Skills

Parents often want their children to develop social skills and an open mindset. Social skills involve the ability to communicate and interact with others. This includes being able to read nonverbal cues, such as body language and facial expressions. It also involves active listening, or paying attention to what the other person is saying and being respectful of others' emotional boundaries.. Parents can help their child develop social skills by modeling these behaviors themselves.

Being open minded means being willing to try new things and to consider other ways of thinking. Parents can encourage their children to be open minded by teaching them about different cultures and lifestyles. They can also expose them to new experiences, such as travel or volunteering.

The next few pages provide material and sample resources that will help you assist your child with identifying and naming their emotions and identifying triggers.

How important is it for you as a parent or guardian to assist your children in developing social skills?

IMPROVING YOUR CHILD'S SOCIAL EMOTIONAL LEARNING SKILLS THROUGH SOCIAL SKILLS

TIP: Talk about bullying with your children. Parents should discourage bullying and watch out for those behaviors by peers who are bullying. Help them differentiate between behaviors that are rude, mean, or bullying.

RUDE, MEAN OR BULLYING?

	rude	mean	bullying
Someone burps loudly nearby	☐	☐	☐
Someone teases you daily about your hair color	☐	☐	☐
Someone laughs at you for wearing the wrong uniform	☐	☐	☐
Someone punches you every day at lunchtime	☐	☐	☐
Someone bumps into you and doesn't say sorry	☐	☐	☐
Someone tells you they don't like the way you smell.	☐	☐	☐

IMPROVING YOUR CHILD'S SOCIAL EMOTIONAL LEARNING SKILLS THROUGH
SOCIAL SKILLS

TIP: Discuss with your children the difference between having a fixed mindset and a growth mindset. Please encourage them to describe moments in their lives when they displayed a fixed attitude or a growth mindset. Discuss the importance of knowing the difference.

MINDSET
YOUR MINDSET DETERMINES YOUR SUCCESS

FIXED MINDSET	GROWTH MINDSET
I already know it all	I want to learn
I give up easily	I welcome and learn from feedback
I ignore useful feedback	I learn from others
I can't change how smart I was born	I can train my brain
I don't need to practice	I will keep trying
Mistakes and failure are bad so I avoid them	Mistakes are learning opportunities
I'll never be good at this	I can work hard to get better at something
I avoid things that require effort	I want to be challenged

KENNETHGAYEDUCATION.COM | @ 2022 KENNETH GAY EDUCATION, LLC

IMPROVING YOUR CHILD'S
SOCIAL EMOTIONAL LEARNING SKILLS THROUGH
SOCIAL SKILLS

TIP: Use this worksheet to complete the Mindset activity.

Growth Mindset Worksheet

NO.	Describe fixed mindset in action	What did you tell yourself (Reflection)	Why did you feel this way (Realisation)
1.			
2.			
3.			
4.			
5.			
6.			
7.			
8.			
9.			

SECTION 4:
TIPS FROM PARENTS JUST LIKE YOU

TIPS FROM PARENTS JUST LIKE YOU.

A small sample of parents, educators, friends and acquaintances were asked the question, "What are 3 things you think parents can do at home to help their child or children develop social emotional learning skills?" The idea is to provide you with tips and suggestions that have worked for other parents-some are hard lessons learned and some are still works in progress. The vignettes used are excepts from The Shoes. Reading the story with your child or even encouraging them to read the story, will provide multiple examples of how we use SEL and to discuss expectations for future behaviors and decision-making.

Provide them with opportunities to interact with others.

> One Thursday in October, I saw some students laugh and talk in hushed voices. I was trying to figure out precisely why all the giggling and laughing. They weren't very disruptive, but I wanted to figure out what was happening. Slyly and keenly observing, I discovered they were laughing at a student's shoes.

How does this vignette apply to the tip? Can you think of ways to describe this scenario or other scenarios to your child?

TIPS FROM PARENTS JUST LIKE YOU.

Teach them to be unique, and comfortable in their own skin with their own personality.

> "I grew up in an African American community where even if you were living in poverty, one way that students ranked themselves as being a little bit better than others was by their shoes. Let me break it down for you. Students may not be able to afford a car to drive, but your shoes are basically like a car. It was a way of showing that you have status, class, and style."

How does this vignette apply to the tip? Can you think of ways to describe this scenario or other scenarios to your child?

TIPS FROM PARENTS JUST LIKE YOU.

Talk kids through their feelings (anger, sadness).

> The student they were making fun of was laughing too. But I could see from his expressions that he was uncomfortable in the situation

How does this vignette apply to the tip? Can you think of ways to describe this scenario or other scenarios to your child?

TIPS FROM PARENTS JUST LIKE YOU.

Be the example and model the behavior they're trying to teach.

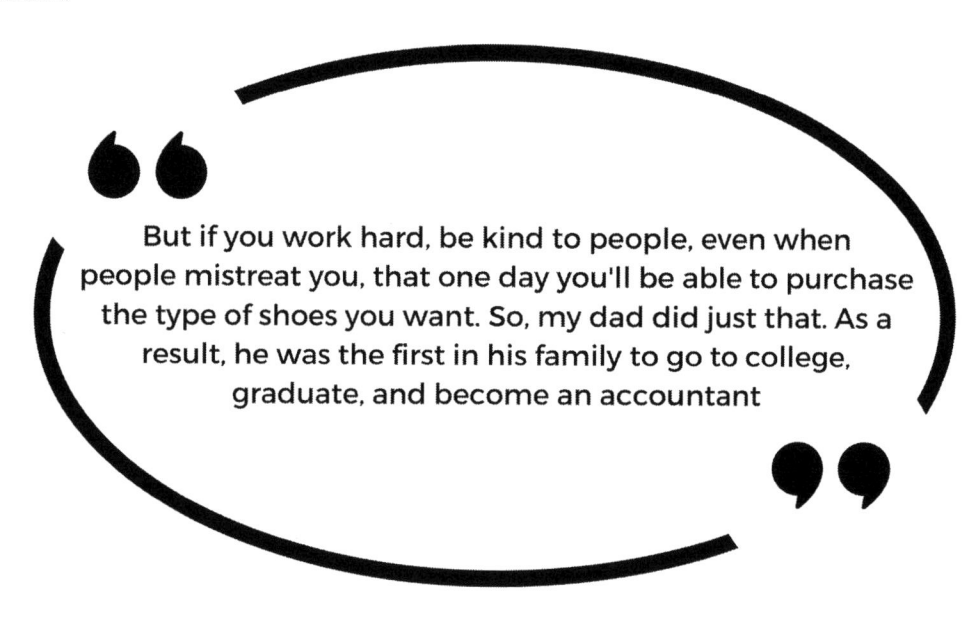

> " But if you work hard, be kind to people, even when people mistreat you, that one day you'll be able to purchase the type of shoes you want. So, my dad did just that. As a result, he was the first in his family to go to college, graduate, and become an accountant "

How does this vignette apply to the tip? Can you think of ways to describe this scenario or other scenarios to your child?

TIPS FROM PARENTS JUST LIKE YOU.

Teaching empathy, discernment and self-worth.

> I shared with the students that sometimes people experience different circumstances in life. For example, you can look around the city and see that some people are poor and some are rich. I shared with them it didn't matter if you started poor. One day, you can become rich. You may even begin rich and one day become poor.

How does this vignette apply to the tip? Can you think of ways to describe this scenario or other scenarios to your child?

TIPS FROM PARENTS JUST LIKE YOU.

Encourage positive relationships with teachers and authority figures.

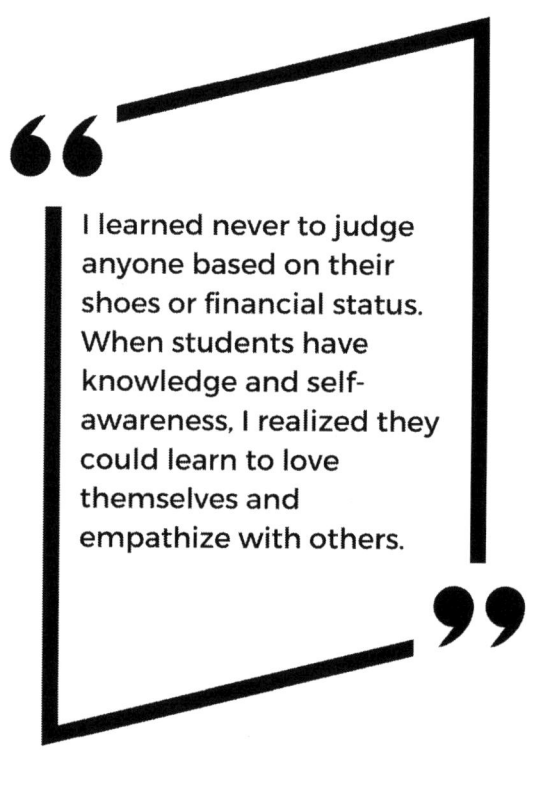

> "I learned never to judge anyone based on their shoes or financial status. When students have knowledge and self-awareness, I realized they could learn to love themselves and empathize with others."

How does this vignette apply to the tip? Can you think of ways to describe this scenario or other scenarios to your child?

TIPS FROM PARENTS JUST LIKE YOU.

Treat children with respect and listen to them.

Think of several ways in which to demonstrate this tip? Write your thoughts here? Reflect on instances when you did a good job or when you could have done better and how?

Ask your child to describe a time when they felt respected and listened to? Also, ask them to communicate what actions make them feel respected.

TIPS FROM PARENTS JUST LIKE YOU.

Respect personal space by not forcing yourself onto another person's body or space without permission.

Think a several ways in which to demonstrate this tip? Write your thoughts here? Reflect on instances when you did a good job or when you could have done better and how?

Ask your child to describe a time when they felt their personal space was or was not being respected. Also, ask them to communicate how the situation could have been improved?

TIPS FROM PARENTS JUST LIKE YOU.

Give kids the appropriate room to fail and help them understand the consequences of their actions.

Think a several ways in which to demonstrate this tip? Write your thoughts here? Reflect on instances when you did a good job or when you could have done better and how?

Ask your child to describe instances when they were given room to make their own decisions and face the consequences of their actions?

TIPS FROM PARENTS JUST LIKE YOU.

Give praise and encouragement often.

Think a several ways in which to demonstrate this tip? Write your thoughts here? Reflect on instances when you did a good job or when you could have done better and how?

Ask your child when and how they would like to be encouraged or praised. (ie openly-in front of others, in private, treats, privileges, etc.)

TIPS FROM PARENTS JUST LIKE YOU.

Put them in situations where they have to respond in different environments.

Think a several ways in which to demonstrate this tip? Write your thoughts here? Reflect on instances when you did a good job or when you could have done better and how?

Describe how your child responded and how you were able to address any issues or questions that arose?

TIPS FROM PARENTS JUST LIKE YOU.

Entrepreneurship can be taught to help them develop their leadership and aptitude as well as mindset.

Think a several ways in which to demonstrate this tip? Write your thoughts here? Reflect on instances when you did a good job or when you could have done better and how?

Entrepreneurship isn't the only way to develop leadership skills. What are some other ways to help your child develop leadership skills?

TIPS FROM PARENTS JUST LIKE YOU.

Allow them to make decisions and hold them accountable.

Think a several ways in which to demonstrate this tip? Write your thoughts here? Reflect on instances when you did a good job or when you could have done better and how?

Ask your child to suggests scenarios and ways they should be held accountable for the decisions they make.

SECTION 5: PARENT/CHILD ACTIVITY-DESIGN YOUR FAVORITE PAIR

PARENT/CHILD ACTIVITY- DESIGN YOUR FAVORITE PAIR

From the Shoes Story, we emphasized presenting shoes from the student's perspective, as demonstrated here:

> "Students may not be able to afford a car to drive, but your shoes are basically like a car. It was a way of showing that you have status, class, and style".

With this quote in mind, you will design your own shoes with your child or separately. The idea here is to have a fun activity to initiate with your children and to set the stage for having, what may be some challenging conversations. This activity will represent time well-spent getting to know your child better and hearing their concerns.

Have fun and enjoy!

Design your favorite pair.

Instructions: Using your imagination, design your favorite pair of shoes.

Design your favorite pair.

Instructions: Using your imagination, design your favorite pair of shoes.

Design your favorite pair.
Instructions: Using your imagination, design your favorite pair of shoes.

Design your favorite pair.
Instructions: Using your imagination, design your favorite pair of shoes.

Design your favorite pair.

Instructions: Using your imagination, design your favorite pair of shoes.

Design your favorite pair.

Instructions: Using your imagination, design your favorite pair of shoes.

Design your favorite pair.

Instructions: Using your imagination, design your favorite pair of shoes.

Design your favorite pair.

Instructions: Using your imagination, design your favorite pair of shoes.

Design your favorite pair.

Instructions: Using your imagination, design your favorite pair of shoes.

Design your favorite pair.

Instructions: Using your imagination, design your favorite pair of shoes.

Design your favorite pair.
Instructions: Using your imagination, design your favorite pair of shoes.

Design your favorite pair.
Instructions: Using your imagination, design your favorite pair of shoes.

Design your favorite pair.
Instructions: Using your imagination, design your favorite pair of shoes.

Design your favorite pair.

Instructions: Using your imagination, design your favorite pair of shoes.

Design your favorite pair.

Instructions: Using your imagination, design your favorite pair of shoes.

Create and design your favorite pair.

Instructions: Using your imagination, create and design your favorite pair of shoes.

Create and design your favorite pair.

Instructions: Using your imagination, create and design your favorite pair of shoes.

Create and design your favorite pair.

Instructions: Using your imagination, create and design your favorite pair of shoes.

Create and design your favorite pair.

Instructions: Using your imagination, create and design your favorite pair of shoes.

Create and design your favorite pair.

Instructions: Using your imagination, create and design your favorite pair of shoes.

Create and design your favorite pair.

Instructions: Using your imagination, create and design your favorite pair of shoes.

SECTION 6:
REFERENCES & CLOSING

REFERENCES

Kankaras, M. (2017), "Personality matter: Relevance and assessment of personality characteristics." OECD Education Working Papers, No. 157, OCED Publishing, https://dx.doi.org/10.1787/8a294376-en

Martinez, Lorea. Teaching with the HEART in Mind: A Complete Educator's Guide to Social Emotional Learning, Kindle Edition, 2021.

A Parent's Resource Guide to Social and Emotional Learning | Edutopia, 2022 https://www.edutopia.org/sel-parents-resources

OECD (2021), Beyond Academic Learning: First Results from the Survey of Social and Emotional Skills, OECD Publishing, Paris, https://doi.org/10.1787/92a11084-en

White, Kisha. Auntie Kisha's Guide: What They Forgot to Tell You Before Your First Day of College, 2022.

CLOSING

Hello Parents!

It has been great having you on this journey with me throughout reading The Shoes: Parent Edition. I hope you were inspired to take action to engage with your child on all levels. I would love you to take time out of your daily routine and continue engaging in deeper conversations with your child about topics in this guide!

The most significant impact happens through:
- Ongoing discussions with your child
- Active listening
- Providing positive feedback
- Restate responses for clarity
- Recognizing when calming thoughts are needed

In the end, I hope you and your child have strengthened your relationship and find it easier to converse about important things. Conversations include discussing relatable topics such as depression or other complicated matters concerning your child. The intent is that they feel more comfortable and supported in sharing their feelings.

I want to thank the students, parents, and teachers who gave feedback.

WIN THE DAY!

Dr. Kenneth R. Gay, Jr.
Founder, Kenneth Gay Education, LLC
kennethgayeducation.com

OTHER BOOKS

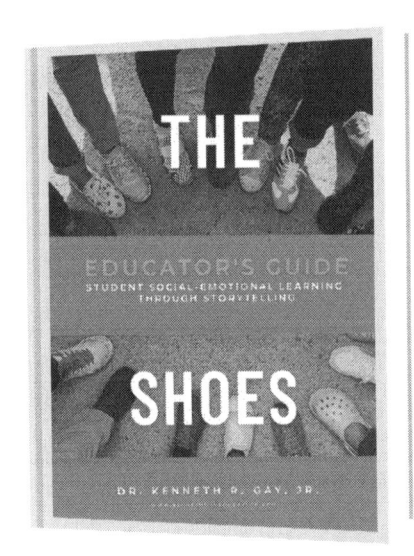

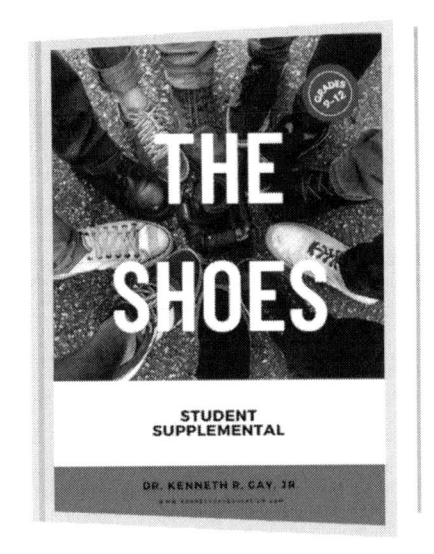

NOW AVAILABLE
amazon

KENNETHGAYEDUCATION.COM | @ 2022 KENNETH GAY EDUCATION, LLC

Made in the USA
Columbia, SC
29 September 2022